Orange and black wings flutter over a field on a sunny summer day. They are the bright wings of a monarch butterfly. The monarch flies from flower to flower. It stops to rest for just a moment. Then it is off again.

The butterfly has laid an egg on a milkweed plant. The egg is about the size of a pencil point. It sparkles in the sunlight like a tiny jewel. This is the first stage in the life of a new monarch butterfly.

A few days later, the egg looks darker. The head of a caterpillar is pushing through the thin shell. The caterpillar is also called a larva. It will crawl out of the egg and onto the plant.

The caterpillar begins eating the moment it hatches. The first thing it eats is the eggshell it just left! After that, it eats only one thing—milkweed leaves.

The caterpillar eats and grows until it can no longer fit inside its tight skin. It must molt, or shed its skin. It leaves its old skin behind and crawls away in a new, looser skin. The caterpillar will molt four or five times in about two weeks.

Then something amazing happens. The caterpillar stops crawling. It even stops eating. Instead, it hangs upside-down from its hind legs. Its skin splits and slides up. Underneath is a hard case. The caterpillar is beginning its next life stage. It is now called a chrysalis, or pupa.

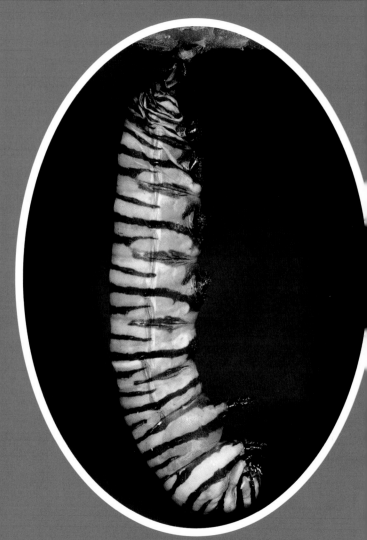

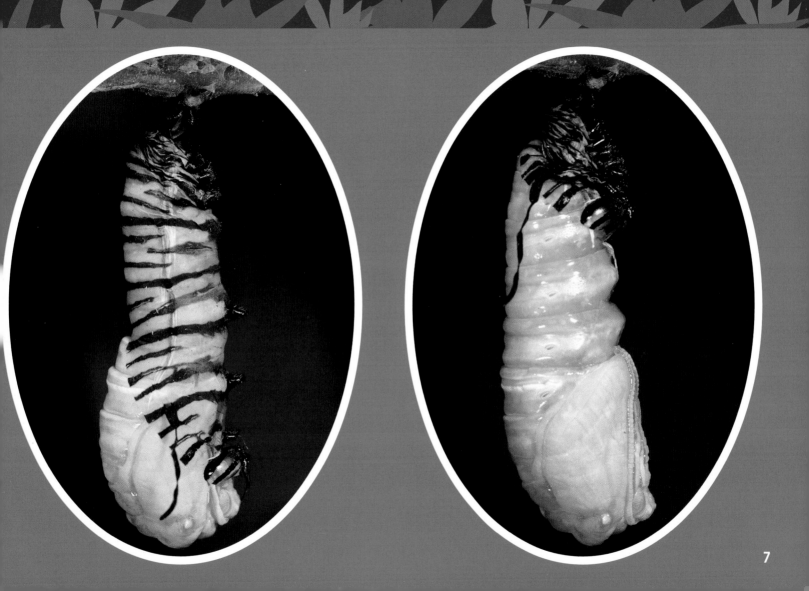

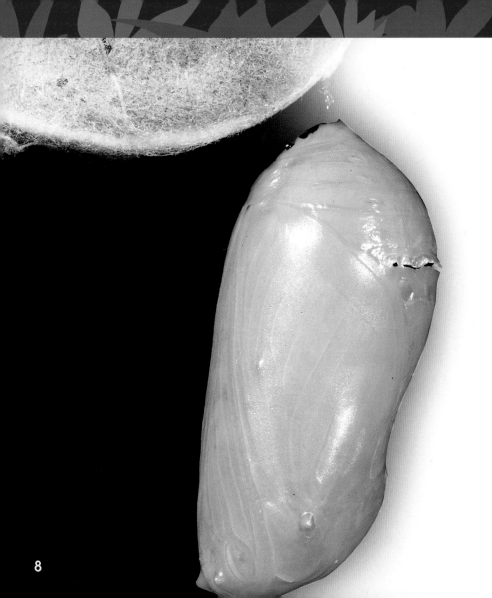

At first the chrysalis is pale green with gold dots. Then the hard case slowly becomes clear. Inside, you can see that the pupa's body has changed. It is turning into an adult butterfly.

The chrysalis splits, and a monarch butterfly crawls out. Its wings are damp and crumpled. They straighten as they slowly fill with blood. The butterfly sits quietly for a few hours as its wings dry and stiffen. Then it flies off.

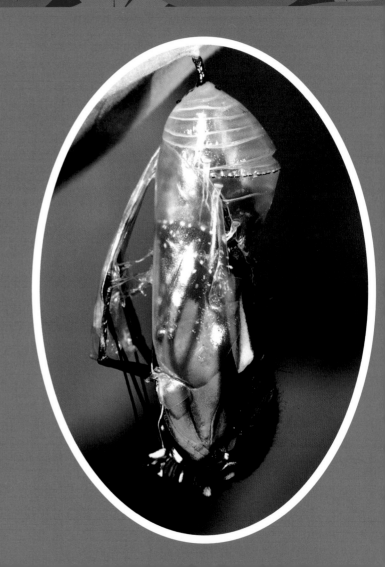

Like its parents, this monarch visits milkweed flowers to feed on nectar. It has gone through all four stages of its life cycle—egg, larva, pupa, and adult—in about a month's time. These changes are called metamorphosis. Now new female butterflies will lay their eggs on milkweed plants, and the monarch life cycle will continue.

Can you put these in order?

Answer

CHOOSE FROM 12 TITLES IN THIS LIFE CYCLES SERIES!

CTP 3059	**Monarch Butterfly**	CTP 3065	**Jumping Spider**
CTP 3060	**Bean**	CTP 3066	**Maple Tree**
CTP 3061	**Sunflower**	CTP 3067	**Green Snake**
CTP 3062	**Wood Frog**	CTP 3068	**Hummingbird**
CTP 3063	**Ladybug**	CTP 3069	**Horse**
CTP 3064	**Chicken**	CTP 3070	**Fighting Fish**

DAVID M. SCHWARTZ

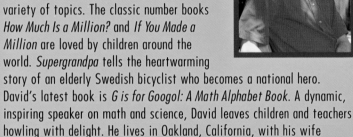

Dale Higgins

David M. Schwartz is an award-winning author of children's books on a wide variety of topics. The classic number books *How Much Is a Million?* and *If You Made a Million* are loved by children around the world. *Supergrandpa* tells the heartwarming story of an elderly Swedish bicyclist who becomes a national hero. David's latest book is *G is for Googol: A Math Alphabet Book*. A dynamic, inspiring speaker on math and science, David leaves children and teachers howling with delight. He lives in Oakland, California, with his wife Yael Schy and their two cats.

DWIGHT KUHN

David Kuhn

Dwight Kuhn is one of the leading nature photographers in America. Artistic close-up images characterize his distinctive style. He became a full-time photographer after eighteen years as a high school chemistry and biology teacher. Dwight's scientific expertise and his artful eye work together with the camera to capture the wonder of the natural world. Textbooks, trade books, and magazines feature Dwight's magnificent photography. He and his family live in Dexter, Maine.

CTP 3059

ISBN 1-57471-579-8

90000

9 781574 715798

0 30554 03059 8

CTP Creative Teaching Press